MW00914895

Walking in Faith

Stories of Hope and
Encouragement for the Workplace

Shari J. Harris

WESTBOW
PRESS
A DIVISION OF THOMAS NELSON

Copyright © 2011 Shari J. Harris

All rights reserved. No part of this book may be used or reproduced by any means, graphic, electronic, or mechanical, including photocopying, recording, taping or by any information storage retrieval system without the written permission of the publisher except in the case of brief quotations embodied in critical articles and reviews.

All Scriptures referenced in this book are from the New International Translation (NIV) Bible.

WestBow Press books may be ordered through booksellers or by contacting:

WestBow Press
A Division of Thomas Nelson
1663 Liberty Drive
Bloomington, IN 47403
www.westbowpress.com
1-(866) 928-1240

Because of the dynamic nature of the Internet, any web addresses or links contained in this book may have changed since publication and may no longer be valid. The views expressed in this work are solely those of the author and do not necessarily reflect the views of the publisher, and the publisher hereby disclaims any responsibility for them.

Any people depicted in stock imagery provided by Thinkstock are models, and such images are being used for illustrative purposes only.

Certain stock imagery © Thinkstock.

ISBN: 978-1-4497-1410-9 (sc)
ISBN: 978-1-4497-1412-3 (hc)
ISBN: 978-1-4497-1411-6 (e)

Library of Congress Control Number: 2011924373

Printed in the United States of America

WestBow Press rev. date: 04/15/2011

In loving memory of my precious, beautiful mother

Darlene Mae Harvatine
1943 – 2010

*Thank you
for always encouraging me,
always believing in me,
and always being a loving
influence in my life.*

You are missed.

*Your legacy of love lives forever
in those you knew and loved.*

*I love you,
Shari Jo*

Whatever you do, work at it with all your heart, as working for the Lord, not men, since you know that you will receive an inheritance from the Lord as a reward. It is the Lord Christ you are serving.

Colossians 3: 23-24

"Let all the brothers, however, preach by their deeds."

St. Francis of Assisi

Contents

Acknowledgements

I would like to thank the following people:

My husband, Bill Harris. Thank you for all your loving support. I could not have completed this project without you.

My son, Chris Harris. Thank you for being my editor and all the hard work this required. You have a gift. Thank you for your support and encouragement.

My friends Jacquie Skog and Leslie Vatne for mentoring, coaching, and encouraging me in my journey through life.

My friends Ann Minter and Kristi Olson for your faithful prayer support.

My friend Tabby Finton for being the first to read my work. Thank you for your contribution to the editing process.

My many friends, too numerous to mention, for all your help, support, encouragement, and prayers along the way.

Lastly, Carie Jones for sharing your faith with me in the workplace.

I am blessed beyond measure to have you in my life.

I love you all.

Author's Note

The following stories chronicle my faith journey in the workplace. I believe God calls us all to take our faith wherever we go, including the workplace. I've been challenged, and I've struggled at work. I haven't always made good choices. My hope in sharing my faith in the workplace stories with you is you will know you are not alone in your struggles. It is my prayer that you will find hope and encouragement in the words that follow.

> *Then Jesus came to them and said, "All authority in heaven and on earth has been given to me. Therefore go and make disciples of all nations, baptizing them in the name of the Father and of the Son and of the Holy Spirit, and teaching them to obey everything I have commanded you. And surely I am with you always, to the very end of the age."*
>
> *Matthew 28:18-20*

Note to Readers

For the most part names have been intentionally been left out to protect those about which I have written. In the few instances where I have used a name, permission was given to me. The names of employers for which I have worked have also been omitted.

The suggested serving size is one story at a time. While the book is short enough to read in one sitting, it is my suggestion you read just one story at a time, taking time to reflect on the Scripture verse associated with each selection.

CHAPTER ONE

Prayer

The Send Me Prayer

*I*t's hard to unexpectedly lose your job. The uncertainty of how lost income will be replaced and how financial obligations will be met can cause much anxiety.

I have been in this uncomfortable situation four times; each time felt more difficult than the previous. I know what it is like to be dislocated from a job and the resulting uncertainty of being unemployed.

I also know God is able to use difficult situations and turn them around and how great things can be the result.

> *And we know that in all things God works for the good of those who love him, who have been called according to his purposes.*
>
> **Romans 8:28.**

My most recent lay-off was in 2003 while working as an office manager for a small technology company. I liked my job. While employed by this company there had been opportunity to form special friendships and to mentor a friend in a life changing way by helping her find her faith. The chance to be involved personally in this type of a relationship was very meaningful to me. I was grateful for the chance and was hopeful of being able to do the same again wherever I went next.

I prayed, *God, send me someplace where You can use me.*

The Send Me Prayer was a sincere prayer from my heart that would be answered in ways I could never have imagined.

My small mind saw God using me to help another individual. God had much bigger plans.

God sent me to a Fortune 500 company, a premier and highly respected employer in my community. While a job was certainly an answer to prayer, the realization of The Send Me Prayer was still ahead.

Armed with no prior knowledge of the term "workplace ministry" I accepted a position on the council of a Christian workplace group only one month after I started with my new employer. This was the beginning of the real journey.

An organized Christian group in the workplace has the potential to help many people. Our group has offered prayer support, Bible studies, faith speakers, and Christian events open to all employees.

I have had a variety of roles and responsibilities on the council's leadership team, including Chairperson, in the last seven years. God is still expanding my responsibilities as He continues to use me. It is a pleasure and privilege to serve God in the workplace.

God continues to surprise me as He allows my workplace ministry role to expand into the community.

God answered The Send Me Prayer by changing a lost job into a whole new direction for my life, giving me a ministry and allowing me to help many people in the workplace.

Then I heard the voice of the Lord saying, "Whom shall I send? And who will go for us?" And I said, "Here am I. Send me!"

Isaiah 6:8

I challenge you to ask God to use you in your workplace. God can change your life through one simple prayer.

Why Did You Wait So Long?

I was in over my head at work again—it certainly wasn't the first time. Demands from my job were mounting, as were my responsibilities as Chairperson of the Christian group. I had some personal concerns weighing me down as well. Barely treading water, I had been fighting going under for weeks, and I didn't know how much longer I could stand the pressure.

It's hard when pressure comes from many sides at the same time.

In desperation, with tears streaming down my face, I asked for prayer at church one Wednesday evening.

"Why did you wait so long to ask for prayer?," a friend asked. The thought-provoking question stopped me cold. Realizing I didn't have an answer was astonishing to me. Looking back, it seems absurd that I waited until the situation was so far out of control before asking for prayer.

Our Savior can move mountains through prayer. As great as my needs felt, they were very small in the hands of God. I wondered, *Why hadn't I asked for prayer?*

In retrospect, there is an answer. In such instances, there is typically a one-word answer—pride. It is pride that prevents us from asking for help. We want the world to think we have it all together, all the time, when nothing could be further from the truth. We tend to want to take care of ourselves and our culture reinforces the idea of individualism.

There is no place in the Bible that instructs us to "do" life alone. God's Word tells us to ask for help—to ask for prayer!

> *Is any one of you in trouble? He should pray. Is anyone happy? Let him sing songs of praise. Is any one of you sick? He should call the elders of the church to pray over him and anoint him with oil in the name of the Lord. And the prayer offered in faith will make the sick person well; the Lord will raise him up. If he has sinned, he will be forgiven. Therefore confess your sins to each other and pray for each other so that you may be healed. The prayer of a righteous man is powerful and effective.*
>
> *James 5:13-16*

God changed my situation through the prayers I'd asked for that night. God changed my attitude with a question from a friend. Prayer is not something I seek only in desperation now, but at the outset of trouble.

Do you need prayer? Don't wait until tomorrow or until the situation is out of control. Ask for prayer today.

There Was the Cross

*T*he words we speak reflect what is in our heart. When we open our mouth our hearts are exposed. Whether we are conscious of it or not, wherever our hearts are focused, this is what we spend our time thinking and talking about. In turn, whatever we are thinking and talking about affects our daily life.

> **As water reflects a face, so a man's heart reflects the man.**
>
> *Proverbs 27:19*

My good friend Jane and I worked at a small technology company. As we shared life together we shared our God stories. We loved to talk about God. We always talked about what God was doing in our life and would often share these stories at work. The conversations were always stimulating, encouraging, and uplifting. It was a joy to run into Jane in the hallway and swap a God story or two in the middle of a busy workday.

Jane and I had made the decision to attend college together, taking a full-time credit load in addition to our full-time jobs and family responsibilities.

It was a stressful time. Work was really busy. School was equally intense. Between work and school our hands were full. At work the company was moving through a high-growth period with each person scrambling to cover the growing demands while additional resources were added. I was working in the Human Resources Department and the pressure was on to hire. At school English Composition class was going to conclude with a big test. The test had a reputation of being tough, and there was added pressure because we needed a minimum score in order to proceed with our program. Jane and I studied feverishly. We began to obsess about the mechanics of grammar. The combined responsibilities of work and school started getting to us.

One morning in quiet reflection, God reminded me to be grateful for my salvation no matter what life circumstances came along. I walked into work that day, found Jane, and exuberantly exclaimed, "Hey Jane, what about our salvation!" I realized my hallway conversations with Jane had turned from Jesus to grammar. In hindsight I saw the more we talked about our worries and concerns, the more they began to weigh us down. I saw the error and the severity of this change, and I wanted to do something about it. With alarm, I suggested we quickly turn our conversations and focus back to Christ.

That evening before class we stopped at the campus chapel as we often did. I stayed on my knees a little longer than usual. I felt the weight of the world on my shoulders. I prayed earnestly for help.

When I opened my eyes there was the cross; it was center-stage and filled my vision. It reminded me to keep my eyes on Jesus and not my circumstances. Just as my physical eyes were opened, so were my spiritual eyes. God indelibly wrote the reminder on my heart that night. Where my thoughts focus influences my life. I needed to make an effort to keep my focus on God.

My step was a little lighter as I walked down the hallway to class; my heart had an extra measure of peace that hadn't been there earlier.

Are you looking at your circumstances today? Change your focus to God by turning your thoughts and conversations to Him.

Praying Friends

As I was settling into my Monday morning work routine, a friend approached me and announced, "I prayed for you on my way to work today." I'm always grateful for prayer, and told her so. It was a great start to the workweek.

Her church had been given a challenge the previous morning; the congregation was asked to pray for someone God placed on each person's heart every day for the coming week.

She had chosen me!

I was blessed to know God put me on her heart. I was comforted to know she was going to be praying for me. My friend's generosity touched me.

"Do you need prayer today?," I recently asked another friend. "Oh, yes, I always need prayer," she quickly replied. That struck me as a very wise answer. Her reply was filled with truth and wisdom.

A wise person knows there is always need for prayer.

And pray in the Spirit on all occasions with all kinds of prayers and requests. With this in mind, be alert and always keep on praying for all the saints.

Ephesians 6:18

God often prompts me to check in with a friend to see if there is a need for prayer only to find a great or immediate reason for prayer support. People are amazed when a friend makes such an offer at just the right moment.

God works that way.

I've been equally as surprised when a friend has done the same for me.

I'm quick to offer prayer to a friend now, knowing what a blessing this can be and knowing how it can meet an immediate need.

Sometimes I ask for a prayer, and other times my amazing friends just pray.

Offer to pray for a friend today. Your friend will be blessed. Ask God who you should bless in this manner, just as my friend did.

Praying for friends in the workplace is a privilege. I love to pray for my friends at work, and I am encouraged to know my friends pray for me.

A Desperate Cry for Help

Celebrating a two-year anniversary in my entry-level position was not something I had envisioned or hoped for. My plan was to spend the required one-year period in the job and then to move on to bigger and better things. I was a year past my critical deadline, and I was exasperated.

The job was not a good fit. I'd taken a big step backward in my career to get into the company with the expectation that I would be able to move on quickly. Coming to work each day was a challenge. Trying to move on had proven to be much more difficult than I had anticipated. Try as I might, no doors were opening.

I sent up a desperate cry for help when I prayed, *I give up, God. I can't do it anymore. If you want me to be here, then I'll be here. But you have to help me be here. I can't do it without you. If I'm supposed to move on you will have to make that happen. Lord, help me.*

I heard God say, *At last —now I can work!*

> **But he said to me, "My grace is sufficient for you, for my power is made perfect in weakness." Therefore I will boast all the more gladly about**

my weaknesses, so that Christ's power may rest on me. That is why, for Christ's sake, I delight in weaknesses, in insults, in hardships, in persecutions, in difficulties. For when I am weak, then I am strong.

2 Corinthians 12:9-10

God can work in me and through me when I throw my hands in the air and let Him have control. Just as the Bible verse says, when I am weak, God is strong.

It is not a coincidence that a new opportunity presented itself shortly after my plea for help. God opened a door. I was able to move through it and on to a much better place for me. The new position gave me more flexibility while giving me the opportunity to use my skills and allowed me to feel like I was making more of a contribution on a daily basis.

God heard my desperate cry for help. He provided me the opportunity I was looking for to move on to another job.

The righteous cry out, and the Lord hears them; he delivers them from all their troubles. The Lord is close to the brokenhearted and saves those who are crushed in spirit.

Psalm 34: 17-18

If you are in a difficult situation, cry out to the Lord. He will hear a desperate cry from your heart just as He heard mine.

CHAPTER TWO

Faith

God Does Not Misdial

A call to leadership can come in a variety of ways. It can come through people as well as circumstances. I was alone in the atrium of my company's world headquarters when God prompted me to step into a leadership position.

I thought the call was a wrong number.

My response was typical. I immediately asked, *Who me, God?* I was sure the call was not mine. I knew it was meant for someone more qualified. So I called someone else.

The Christian group, on which I was a council member, was without a leader. I didn't want to panic, but I needed to act quickly. I called Glenn because he led the group through a crisis the previous year. The Christian group may or may not have been in another crisis, but I was for sure!

"I'll pray about it," was Glenn's promise. He was leaving on a trip with his family and assured me he would call back upon his return. I knew Glenn was a man of his word, and I was comforted knowing he would make it a matter of prayer.

Two weeks didn't pass quickly enough. When the return call came, Glenn apologetically explained that he did not feel God was calling him to take the helm again. I was disappointed; however, I was not surprised.

"That's okay, Glenn. I know who God is calling," I responded. I knew God had asked me.

After thanking Glenn for his consideration, I let God know I was willing to listen and go wherever He wanted me to go and do whatever He wanted me to do. I reminded God I didn't feel qualified for what He was asking. He knew.

God knew I doubted myself, and that I should not doubt Him.

I was about to learn that God doesn't necessarily call the qualified, but that He does qualify the called.

It is never a wrong number when God calls. God does not misdial.

> *Jude, a servant of Jesus Christ and a brother of James, To those who have been called, who are loved by God the Father and kept by Jesus Christ: Mercy, peace and love be yours in abundance.*
>
> *Jude 1:1-2*

I have been abundantly blessed through answering God's call.

Turn On the Light

"Even in the dark there is light." Those words from a song wafting through the radio airwaves caught my attention, and my mind raced back to a conversation on work I had with a friend the previous evening. As she recounted her work story from the day, my heart went out to her; she'd encountered such darkness.

But her heart was not heavy. My friend's heart was full of hope as she told me how God had given her grace and a light heart to deal with the situation.

Even in the dark there is light. The light is Christ, and because we bring Him with us we can *be* light in the darkness.

> *"You are the light of the world. A city on a hill cannot be hidden. Neither do people light a lamp and put it under a bowl. Instead they put it on its stand, and it gives light to everyone in the house. In the same way, let your light shine before men, that they may see your good deeds and praise your Father in heaven."*
>
> *Matthew 5:14-16*

Jesus calls us to be a light everywhere we go. The workplace needs light desperately, and we are called to bring it. With the number of hours many of us spend working, where else do we have the potential to have a greater impact?

If you are known as a Christian, chances are good that your coworkers are watching your behavior. We can choose to be a good example and model godly character or a bad example. Our actions can be a powerful testimony. When we love our coworkers who are not treating us well, we are light in a dark world. God's light shines right through when we bring joy and peace into our workplaces.

> *You are all sons of the light and children of the day.*
> *We do not belong to the night or to the darkness.*
> *So then, let us not be like others, who are asleep,*
> *but let us be alert and self-controlled.*
>
> *1 Thessalonians 5: 5-6*

It is really easy to fall into behaviors that don't honor God when everyone else is modeling them and even encouraging such behavior in others. It can be a tough choice to react differently. But, with God's grace, it's possible.

My friend let light into a dark place when she responded to a negative situation with grace.

The workplace can be dark, but even in the darkness there is light. When we make the choice to positively impact negative situations, we are allowing God's light into the darkness. We are not alone. God is with us. Turn on the light today.

Stormy Weather

hen the weatherman on the nightly news predicts stormy weather, we have an idea of what to expect. Although we may not know the exact timing, the meteorologists are likely to give us a good idea of when the storm will hit and its intensity. Unless, of course, we choose not to listen to the news or heed the storm warnings, we can plan for the weather and adjust plans accordingly

We often don't have the luxury of advance warning when the storms of life begin blowing. Such was the case when I started my new job. New beginnings are often pleasant, and I had no reason to expect anything else. A storm of life came up without warning, or if there were any warning signs I missed them completely.

My initial instinct is always to pray the storm away, *God, please take the unpleasantness away! I want to be warm, dry, and safe—comfortable at all times.*

I prayed and prayed. The storm raged on and on. Day after day the winds buffeted me until a day when God captured my attention through the words of a song on the radio. The words from a Scott Krippayne[1] song spoke tenderly to my current condition saying, "Sometimes He calms the storm, and other times He calms His child."

I was supposed to let God calm me *in* the storm! I wasn't going to pray the storm away. That wasn't what God wanted me to do. God wanted me to learn to let Him quiet me during the storm. I was supposed to find peace *while* the winds raged.

This was a new idea. I began to pray in a different way. I began to pray for peace in the storm.

Something changed and I did find peace in the middle of the difficult circumstances.

> **Without warning, a furious storm came up on the lake, so that the waves swept over the boat. But Jesus was sleeping. The disciples went and woke him, saying, "Lord, save us! We're going to drown!" He replied, "You of little faith, why are you so afraid?" Then he got up and rebuked the winds and the waves, and it was completely calm.**
>
> **Matthew 8: 24-26**

God can still calm stormy weather. However, sometimes that is not in our best interest. There are life lessons that can only be learned when the rain is pelting us.

We can find peace, with Jesus Christ, in stormy weather and in all circumstances.

Once I let God calm me in the storm, my outlook changed and so did the stormy weather—the skies began to clear and so did my vision.

The lesson stayed with me. Sometimes God does calm the storm, and sometimes we need to let Him calm us in the middle of stormy weather.

Lunchtime Prayers

We bowed our heads in prayer, asking God to bless our time together and the meal we were about to share. My friend and I were having lunch in the cafeteria where we work. Our busy schedules seldom intersect, and lunch together was always a welcome treat.

It's a pleasure to see my friend. She always has a smile and a warm hug. In the middle of a hectic workday these things are heartwarming and uplifting.

We both happened to have heavy hearts for individual work situations that day, each of us struggling with something in our jobs—the struggle of working with people when we do not always understand each other.

God spoke to each of us in an individual and personal way as we shared our work struggles, using the other to shed light and give insight into the situations at hand. It felt good to share my concerns. My friend felt the same.

> *Carry each other's burdens, and in this way you will fulfill the law of Christ.*
>
> *Galatians 6:2*

Admitting I had not handled my part of my current situation well, I asked for prayer. It was not easy to admit and own up to my part in the misunderstanding, but it was helpful.

> *Therefore confess your sins to each other and pray for each other so that you may be healed. The prayer of a righteous man is powerful and effective.*
>
> *James 5:16*

We were both given revelation in how to respond differently to our not-so-different challenges. God worked through each of us to minister to the other.

We parted company promising to keep each other in prayer.

Immediately upon returning to work I saw a glimmer of hope in the situation over which my heart was heavy. The coworker my friend and I had just prayed for asked me to help her with a problem. I was grateful for the chance to respond by helping her.

Do you have a friend whose prayers seem to impact your life in a powerful way? God has blessed me with special friends whose prayers have changed my life in countless situations.

The key ingredient is the love inserted into their prayers. I can pray like crazy for myself, as I had been doing in this situation. However, it was when I opened my heart, shared my concerns, and let my friend who loves me pray, that God really was able to move in a powerful way. Prayers from a heart of love change the world. Lunchtime prayers can change the course of your day.

Called to the Workplace

"I'll go where you send me," the words from the song at church struck a strong chord of remembrance deep in my heart.

I had not completely forgotten this; however, my vision had become clouded with doubt in the middle of current work challenges. Life can be tough and that is no time to forget your purpose. I was thankful for the reminder of how I was called to my workplace. The song's timing was perfect. It was a message I needed to hear.

I started college as an adult. Choosing a Christian institution was significant in my spiritual walk and development. I was very pleased with the opportunity to study in a Christian environment; daily devotions, prayer, and Christian fellowship were part of the program. I enjoyed looking at each subject through the biblical lens the school required for each area of study. My general education electives were Bible based, and I loved them!

My fellow students and professors frequently asked me why I wasn't in the ministry program. Oh, how I longed to be! My heart was to follow after God and to serve Him. Although I was able to give a quick answer, I struggled with the question for several years.

I was in the business program, knowing God was asking me to be in the business world. There is a strong need for Christian men and women in every vocation. It's imperative for Christians to be in the marketplace, where people do not always have faith, demonstrating good values and ethics.

God calls people to the traditional ministry field. I am thankful He does and that people are willing to serve in the church and on the mission fields.

However, it is also important to realize God calls us into the workplace as well.

I had felt unprepared for the assignment of being a Christ-follower in the work environment. I remembered reminding myself that God knew where He asked me to be, that He equipped me, and that God goes with me.

It isn't in *my* strength God works, but through *His* strength. I don't have to have confidence in who I am, but I can have every confidence in Christ.

I think of God's disciples and what a motley crew they were. They were ordinary men with faults and weaknesses too. Ken Blanchard, co-author of *Lead Like Jesus*[2], wrote, "I became fascinated with how Jesus transformed twelve ordinary and unlikely people into the first generation of leaders of a movement that continues to affect the course of world history some two thousand years later."

Am I still willing to go wherever God sends me, even if it's the corporate work world? I thought, *But God, it can be so dark there!*

Yes, I am willing to go.

I love Mary's response when God called on her.

"I am the Lord's servant," Mary answered. "May it be to me as you have said."

Luke 1:38

Do you feel ordinary? It's okay. God can use you in the workplace if you are willing.

Faith Believes

When I don't see God's plan unfolding in my life, it doesn't mean there is not a plan. God always has a strategy and He's always working out the details.

My life, including my time spent at work, overflows with His abundance. When I have doubtful moments, God's blessings are still all around me, and the biggest one yet may be around the next corner. I have to trust. I have to have faith.

> *Trust in the Lord with all your heart and lean not on your own understanding; in all your ways acknowledge to him, and he will make your paths straight.*
>
> *Proverbs 3: 5-6*

On a recent fall trip, as my family and I marveled at God's beauty revealed through the changing foliage, God gave me an illustration of faith.

The trees were spectacular, more brilliant than I'd remembered seeing in years. I felt incredibly blessed and couldn't believe God would have timed our trip to coincide perfectly with nature's performance; for surely it was the precise moment of peak colors displayed that day, seemingly just for us!

Looking ahead I saw a particularly colorful patch of trees on a hillside. I fixed my eyes on the delightful scenery, anticipating the visual treat a closer view was going to bring. Much to my dismay, the road suddenly curved and a hillside cropped up completely blocking my view. I stared longingly at the barren hillside as it rushed past outside the car window.

It made me think of a work situation. An exciting opportunity I was looking forward to seemed lost. Although I was counting on an expected event happening, the opportunity had disappeared from my view. Doubt clouded my vision so much that I'd lost all hope of seeing what was once so clearly in my line of sight. A friend woke me up from my doubt-induced stupor by challenging me with, "Oh, ye of little faith."

As we passed the obstacle on that fall drive, God's splendor was displayed in full view. Much to my surprise, I had not missed the vivid scenery I was anticipating. God had timed it such that I had a front row seat, from a perfect vantage point, at just the right moment.

God reminded me the beautiful trees were still there when the hillside temporarily blocked my vision, just as the work opportunity was still there hidden behind current circumstances.

Nothing could change the fact the trees existed beyond what my eyes could see. Just as the spectacular fall scenery was always there, so is God's good plan for me. It was several months before I saw the possibility at work again, but it was there just as the trees on the trip had been.

"For I know the plans I have for you," declares the Lord, "plans to prosper you and not to harm you, plans to give you hope and a future."

Jeremiah 29:11

God has the perfect plan for each one of us. Faith believes this even when our eyes do not see it. It was several more months, but the hoped for opportunity became reality. Faith believes God at all times.

CHAPTER THREE

Relationships

God's Hand at Work

I am thankful for the assistance God has provided me through friends. Many friends have served as mentors, coaches, and personal advisors. I am grateful for each precious friend and the contributions they have made in my life. These men and women have served as role models helping me learn and grow, supporting me in good times and bad.

The connection point for these beautiful relationships has often been the workplace. Friendships started there have flourished into deep and lasting relationships that have been a source of comfort, strength, and encouragement as well as guidance.

With a sudden realization of *how* many great mentors God has provided me, I recently began to wonder . . .

When will I not need so much help, God?

Never —was the clear, firm, concise response. Just one word; God did not need to elaborate. In my heart I already knew this was the right answer.

God created us to need each other. God works through us. His design for us is to lean on each other. We are not supposed to walk the road of life alone. We are supposed to reach out to each other, giving and receiving love. God's design was deliberate and purposeful—the plan allowing God to work through us.

When you see the outstretched hand of a friend, don't hesitate to reach back; it is God's hand reaching toward you.

Many people spend the majority of their hours in the workplace. What better place might there be to interact and connect, to give and receive encouragement? Work demands and stress are high. We need each other in the workplace. We need to see God's hand at work.

Reach out to another in your office today and offer a few words of encouragement. Take the hand you see outstretched in your direction. It's God's hand reaching out to touch you.

> *Therefore encourage one another and build each other up, just as in fact you are doing.*
> *1 Thessalonians 5:11*

Thank you, my friends, your love and support mean the world to me. I pray God richly blesses you.

Relationships Matter

I don't have five minutes for you," my friend told me. "I have a new project and I'm going to be busy." Ouch. We were pretty good friends, or so I thought. This was rather abrupt. Sure, work had gotten pretty crazy for everyone, but this was really confusing. Stunned I mumbled something about lunch and weekends. She quickly let me know that she was going to be so busy she wouldn't have time for lunch or be able to connect on the weekends either. She was going to be tired from being so busy and would need her lunch hours, if she ever got one, and weekends to rest.

Whether I reached out to her as a colleague or a friend, she was true to her word and insistence she couldn't spare even a few minutes.

Busy is an interesting word today. I hear it everywhere. We are all *busy—too busy*—all the time. The funny thing is, we all have twenty-four hours in our day, nothing more, nothing less. That's the way it's always been. What has changed? What are we all too busy doing? And why are we so intent on being so busy? People often brag about how busy they are, as if more activity equates to importance somehow.

The words *too busy* become a cop-out. We hide behind the excuse of being busy, such in the case of my friend. Obviously there was much more going on than a new project. We think pleading too busy protects us from harm by helping us avoid situations in which we would rather not deal.

Jesus was never too busy, nor should we be. Relationships matter a great deal to God. He wants relationships to be important to us too. The only way to nurture a relationship is to devote time.

Where each of us spends our given minutes each day speaks to our priorities.

We all know a dying person is not going to lament, "I wish I would have spent more time at work!"

Henri Nouwen, author of *In the Name of Jesus[3]*, states, "Beneath all the great accomplishments of our time there is a deep current of despair. While efficiency and control are the great aspirations of our society, the loneliness, isolation, lack of friendship and intimacy, of emptiness and depression, a deep sense of uselessness fill the hearts of millions of people in our success-oriented world."

Being too busy isolates people and feeds into the current of despair. A *too busy life* dams the flow of the Holy Spirit.

Resting in Jesus is our only hope for restoring order in a chaotic world. More activity only contributes to the chaos. Once we learn to rest in Christ, our relationships with others will naturally improve.

"Remain in me, and I will remain in you. No branch can bear fruit by itself; it must remain in the vine. Neither can you bear fruit unless you remain in me."

John 15:4

We choose our level of busy. We don't have to be too busy. We can choose to rest in Jesus. We can't be busy and rest at the same time. We can choose to invest our time in relationships knowing they matter a great deal.

Busiest Girl in the Office

She rushes past your desk each morning, barely able to mumble a cursory "good morning," as she zooms by. There is no reason to do more than hurriedly gush the same in reply; anything else would be lost in her dust. There is no time for pleasantries. She has important work to do.

She wears her busyness proudly, boasting of it, displaying it as if it were a medal pinned on her lapel. Although too busy to ask how you are, she'll stop for just a moment if you want to admire her busy badge. She's very proud of it. She's worked very hard for it.

Oh, but there are deadlines to meet, projects to complete; the company is on her shoulders, or so she seems to think. Although she's given you a moment, it's far more time than she has to spare.

Do you know her? She's the busiest girl in the office.

She never takes a coffee break or accepts an invitation to lunch. She's much too busy for meaningless chatter. She's busy, you know. You will find her at the company function in the evening though; she wouldn't miss a chance to tell her superiors how busy and important she is.

The busiest girl in the office takes great care in choosing her attire and in grooming. The perception of perfection is part of the plan. A good façade is part of the masquerade.

Her lips sing her own praises and laud her work; but there is something in her eyes. Is it pain? Is it loneliness? No one knows.

Her smile never wanes—it is one of the brightest, albeit highly artificial, in the office.

My heart goes out to the busiest girl in the office because I once was her. I gave it my all at the office, pouring myself into my job, putting work above everything else—above *everyone* else.

Accolades from the boss were wonderful; yet, something was missing. I was feeling empty inside. Always with a bright (perhaps even the brightest smile in the office) I pushed on.

The day I discovered I was running from myself and working so hard to cover my pain, was the day I was able to let God change me. It was the day I was able to let Him begin healing my hurting heart. I was able to take a breath, stop running, and quit pretending.

Work cannot fill our heart with peace and joy—only God can do this.

Jobs are important, but they are not the most important thing in life; they come and go. God, family, and friends are forever.

I lost the job where I was trying to lose myself; but in the process I found myself. I'm grateful I didn't lose my family and friends.

Pray for the busiest girl in the office. She may be the person in greatest need.

May the God of hope fill you with all joy and peace as you trust in him, so that you may overflow with hope by the power of the Holy Spirit.

Romans 15:13

Impostor!

$\mathcal{T}$he smile is quick and bright when you meet; however she turns it off as fast as she rounds the corner—her happy expression turns to a snicker, her scowl reflects her scorn. She hides behind the smile, but her words give her away. Her actions are inconsistent with the air of pleasantness she tries to present. Something in her eyes does not match her smile. There is a feeling of hostility draping her shoulders like a cape and the air is heavy in her wake.

She is an impostor. Under the façade is a wounded, hurting soul. The woman is so critical and judgmental because hurting people have a tendency to hurt other people.

I wish we could stop the pretense. Conditioned to pretend we give a perfunctory "fine" whenever asked how we are. We smile through pain and all kinds of challenges, never admitting our struggles or fear.

Afraid of being exposed as less than perfect, fear can drive us to act in strange, often destructive ways.

We need to be honest—first with ourselves and then with others. People are hungry for authenticity.

I don't want to lie about who I am. I don't want anyone to say of me, "Imposter!" I'm broken, hurting, challenged and struggling too. Admitting this allows me to be genuine and gives others freedom to do the same.

In *Beautiful Things Happen When A Women Trusts God*[4], speaker and author Shelia Walsh stated, "Suddenly I began to see that my brokenness was a far greater bridge to others than my pretend wholeness had ever been."

When we are genuine and real, we give others permission to be the same. Pretending to be perfect isn't fooling anyone, nor is it helping anyone. Healing starts when our fears, faults and weaknesses are exposed, because it is in the dark they fester and hold us hostage. We are responsible for this exposure; it is necessary to stop the hurt and in turn the fear-driven behavior.

Walsh wrote, "I began to see that when we keep our fears and wounds in the dark night of solitude, they never have a chance to heal; but when we share our pain, we invite others to come out of the darkness into the light of Christ for healing and hope."

> *The Spirit of the Sovereign Lord is on me, because the Lord has anointed me to preach good news to the poor. He has sent me to bind up the brokenhearted, to proclaim freedom for the captives and release from darkness for the prisoners, to proclaim the year of the Lord's favor and the day of vengeance of our God, to comfort all who mourn, and provide for those who grieve in Zion—to bestow on them a crown of beauty instead of ashes, the oil of gladness instead of mourning, and a garment of praise instead of*

a spirit of despair. They will be called oaks of righteousness, a planting of the Lord for the display of his splendor.

Isaiah 61:1-3

God desires to heal our wounds. Ask Him today what He wants you to confess and expose to the light. Sharing it with a friend may do more than set you free; your friend may be set free too.

Not Made for Perfection

*A*s my journey takes me down many corporate America corridors, I observe a sea of people trying to conform, so much so they almost begin to look alike. Nearly identically dressed men and women rush by me in an endless stream.

In the movie *The Stepford Wives*, the men of Stepford, Connecticut all had submissive, impossibly beautiful and perfect wives. They appeared to be perfect because the women were robots. The people I pass at work sometimes remind me of the zombie-like women in the movie. While both look great on the outside, there is something devoid of life behind the shiny exteriors.

There is a desperate clamor to be perfect, expressed by the willingness to conform to one standard. Perfect attire. Flawless hair. Unblemished make-up. Complete this picture with a perfect smile, although often perfectly false. I see it every day.

Are we trying to cover up the fact we are not perfect? God knows our hearts. He created us.

> *O Lord, you have searched me and you know me. You know when I sit and when I rise; you perceive my thoughts from afar. You discern my*

going out an my lying down; you are familiar
with all my ways. Before a word is on my tongue
you know it completely, O Lord.

Psalm 139: 1-4

Not one of us can boast perfection. Let us confess our imperfection, sin, and brokenness to God, who already knows everything about us, and then to each other. We all hunger for the chance to be who God created us to be— unique, although imperfect, beautiful children of God.

In *Beautiful Things Happen When A Woman Trusts God* by Sheila Walsh, this beautiful woman of God shares her story of pain buried deep beneath a perfect exterior. She wrote, "I always thought that people wanted me to be perfect so I could help them. If I reached out for help myself, I had reasoned, that I would lose my perceived usefulness."

It's time to stop the pretense. It's time to bust the misconception that we are all supposed to be without a flaw.

Walsh wrote, "But the truth is, all I have to offer anyone else is a life surrendered to Christ so that His beauty and grace shines through my brokenness."

The greatest gift we can give each other is a willingness to share our imperfection and accept each other just the way we are. There is freedom in such a gift. It's okay to be different. God created us to be individuals, each with our own personalities and styles. We were not made for perfection. It's in our imperfection that God has a chance to use us to minister to each other. Look deeply within yourself and see your own uniqueness, and dare to be yourself at work. In doing so you may just give another person permission to do the same.

CHAPTER FOUR

Forgiveness

Guard Your Heart

Above all else, guard your heart, for it is the wellspring of life.

Proverbs 4:23

What does "guard your heart" mean? Does it mean you cannot share your heart with anyone? Or does it caution care when you do?

Sharing your heart anytime can be risky and scary—such an act can be even more so at work.

I recently shared my tears with a new friend at work, one I had deemed trustworthy of such precious cargo, only to be hurt.

My friend and I shared tears with each other, and then she shared mine with another coworker. This information sharing would have been a hurtful act of betrayal even if the tears had been broadcast with accuracy; however, the tears were grossly misinterpreted and relayed inaccurately. The version shared was misconstrued, based loosely on one unrelated comment to the tearful confessions of my heart.

It hurt to find out what had been said about me. It wasn't true. The coworker hearing the wrong version was a friend who knew me far better than to put any value in the incorrect words that were repeated to her. I was at least thankful for that.

The comments made were not just hurtful personally, but also had the potential to negatively impact me professionally. Was the act of betrayal done with malicious intent, or was it an innocent mistake? I trusted the latter, brought up to always give the benefit of the doubt. But in the days following I saw a self-centered, climb-the-ladder-to-success-no-matter-who-you-need-to-step-on side of this person leading me to question motive. I also learned of how many in the office she had conflict with because of the same reason. Even so, it was hard not to take it personally.

I may never know the answer to my question. With an act of finality she closed the curtain of our friendship, not allowing any conversation or a chance to mend the fence. She built a fortress around herself as if her heart were the one betrayed.

Try as I might for permission to reenter, even a chance for a conversation was repeatedly denied. Many attempts to reconcile failed, leaving me mystified as to what really happened and how another could be so hard and difficult.

> *If it is possible, as far as it depends on you, live*
> *at peace with everyone.*
> *Romans 12:18*

My best attempts to reconcile were in vain and there was nothing else I could do but pray for her. There is something that I don't know and understand, but God does. He can heal broken hearts.

Stinging from such a hurtful betrayal, it is easy to want to build a fortress around my own heart as a response. My natural inclination is to never trust again.

God does not want to see this happen.

The better response to hurt and betrayal is in learning to only let in a trusted few. Guard your heart; but do not seal it off. Just take care with whom you share your heart with. High levels of trust should be saved for others who also know Christ, and not friends who do not share a faith in Jesus.

We should give Jesus our broken heart for healing, and then continue on, in the name of Jesus, to trust again. God is relational and desires us to be in relationships with each other.

Right Heart

What had started out as a simple misunderstanding with a coworker had ballooned into something much more. Hard feelings had developed somewhere along the line as the situation wasn't addressed. It had gone on for too long. I had prayed countless prayers and asked others to pray for me too.

A couple of things happened to turn the situation around.

Coming back from a prayer breakfast, I shared my concerned heart with a group of my Christian friends. Right in front of my workplace, as they were dropping me off, my friends and I joined hands and they earnestly prayed for my circumstances. I felt the prayers were powerful before I even stepped out of the van and walked back through the front door.

Back at my desk I busied myself with the tasks at hand.

Later that day God showed me that my heart had not been right all along when I prayed all those earlier prayers. I'd been praying out of a sense of duty, doing it only because I was supposed to—not because I wanted to do what was right. I had been praying for the other person, but my heart was really focused on me.

Angry with my coworker, I had stopped praying out of a heart of love. I had been praying for the situation between us to change because I wanted rescued from an uncomfortable situation.

God showed me a picture of a little girl, sullen with her arms tightly crossed, spitting out the word "sorry" only because her mother was forcing her to apologize to her brother. The child's insincerity was sorely evident.

I was convicted. I was that little girl.

> *"But I tell you: Love your enemies and pray for those who persecute you, that you may be sons of your Father in heaven. He causes his sun to rise on the evil and the good, and sends rain on the righteous and the unrighteous. If you love those who love you, what reward will you get? Are not even the tax collectors doing that? And if you greet only your brothers, what are you doing more than others? Do not even pagans do that? Be perfect, therefore, as your heavenly Father is perfect."*
>
> *Matthew 5:44-48*

God opened my eyes and my changed my heart. I didn't want to be that sullen little girl.

> *The Lord is far from the wicked but he hears the prayer of the righteous.*
>
> *Proverbs 15:29*

Prayers change the world. Prayers of love from pure hearts have the power to dramatically change circumstances and herald in miracles. God is Love; and He works through love.

Dear friends, let us love one another, for love comes from God. Everyone who loves has been born of God and knows God. Whoever does not love does not know God, because God is love.

1 John 4:7-8

Little did I know that God was going to use the prayers of my friends to change me. I am glad God showed me how important it was to pray with a right heart.

We can change our workplaces prayer at a time. There is power in prayer.

Heart Condition

The human heart is a mystery. Science is able to study the inner workings of this intricate organ and understands its physiology. The intrigue comes when we look at the heart as the keeper of our emotions. For example, what does it mean when we say our heart "aches"? It's not a physical pain we refer to, but an emotional discomfort.

Take forgiveness—a matter of the heart, no doubt. Forgiving can be a very difficult matter for the heart, and it can be the source of much heartache. My brain is intelligent enough to understand the concept of forgiveness and the wisdom too. It seems simple enough for my head. My intellect can even give me proper instructions to go through the process. Alas, my heart is not so smart. Sometimes it doesn't want to listen to what is right, and would rather respond like a small child. When my heart aches it is very stubborn and unwilling to listen to reason. My heart holds onto anger and bitterness long after my head has been able to process a hurtful event and give good reason to dismiss the negative emotions associated with being unforgiving.

For if you forgive other men when they sin against you, your heavenly Father will also forgive you. But if you do not forgive men their sins, your Father will not forgive your sins.

Matthew 6: 14-15

Wow. My head "gets" it. If I don't forgive those who cause me harm, God is not going to forgive me. That is a serious problem!

I do not understand what I do. For what I want to do I do not do, but what I hate I do. And if I do what I do not want to do, I agree that the law is good. As it is, it is no longer I myself who do it, but it is sin living in me. I know that nothing good lives in me, that is, in my sinful nature. For I have the desire to do what is good, but I cannot carry it out. For what I do is not the good I want to do; no, the evil I do not want to do--this I keep on doing. Now if I do what I do not want to do, it is no longer I who do it, but it is sin living in me that does it.

Romans 7:15-20

Then why does my heart not respond more appropriately and make better choices? We have a heart condition. The diagnosis is serious. The problem is sin.

Forgiving each other is not an option; it is a command. Forgiving can be very challenging. However, it is what God calls us to do. God does not leave us to this difficult task on our own, but has given us the power of the Holy Spirit.

"But the Counselor, the Holy Spirit, whom the Father will send in my name, will teach you all things and will remind you of everything I have

said to you. Peace I leave with you; my peace I give you. I do not give to you as the world gives. Do not let your hearts be troubled and do not be afraid."

John 14: 26-27

I will never understand the way the heart works as keeper of the emotions. The heart keeps us alive, both physically and emotionally. Perhaps this is all I need to understand; maybe the emotional side is not one we are meant to understand.

A heart condition is a serious matter. I must turn this fascinating organ and the condition of my heart over to God, admitting my heart condition, and surrendering it to Him.

Misunderstood

*T*he sinking feeling in my stomach and heaviness in my chest were both confirmation—I was hearing something I didn't want to hear, didn't want to be true, and it was definitely from God.

I swallowed hard, closed my eyes, and whispered a quick prayer.

Have you ever been misunderstood? I have and it's not much fun.

The feeling and desire to ignore what I was hearing from God came as I was preparing for a meeting in which I hoped someone would be willing to give me a second chance. The person I was about to meet with had misunderstood me. She had been given wrong information and I knew she had believed it.

I began to wonder, *What if. . .?*

What if I'd been wrong and totally misjudged someone the same way I had been wrongly accused? What if that person really hadn't meant to hurt me and I had misunderstood actions, words, and motives? I knew from being on the other end that it can easily happen, and it might happen far more often and easily than I think.

The whispered prayer was asking God to help me accept I had been wrong and for help in forgiving the person I had likely misunderstood.

I knew I couldn't do it in my own strength. I'd been hurt too badly, had harbored bitterness in my heart too long. I needed God's help.

> *"Do not judge, or you too will be judged. For in the same way you judge others, you will be judged, and with the measure you use, it will be measured to you."*
>
> *Matthew 7:1-2*

I was being judged to the same degree I judged my coworker, and it didn't feel very good.

> *"For if you forgive men when they sin against you, your heavenly Father will also forgive you. But if you do not forgive men their sins, your Father will not forgive your sins."*
>
> *Matthew 6: 14-15*

What if I didn't forgive my coworker?

There was far too much at stake not to listen to what I was hearing.

I heard the voice of the coworker God was speaking to me about in the next cube corridor and wondered if God was going to guide her footsteps past me. She was someone I seldom saw; yet, God guided her footsteps right across my path in the next moment.

Only God could have orchestrated the timing. Only God could have filled my heart with goodness and given me the gumption to put my ego aside and be nice to the one that had hurt me.

CHAPTER FIVE

Hope

Out Of Balance

What thoughts spring to your mind when the phrase *corporate America* is mentioned? I confess my first thought is *out-of-balance*. Subsequent thoughts aren't any better. I think of stress, struggles, challenges, negative coworkers, unreasonable expectations, and increasingly higher demands. I think of how down-sizing has created an expectation to accomplish the same, if not more results, with increasingly less resources. It seems that employees are being stretched as far as can be, and stress is at an all-time high. I think of how technology has allowed us to have our minds on work around the clock, and how unhealthy it is to never unplug from work. The current atmosphere and culture in my workplace seems more than out-of-balance; it feels broken and out-of-order.

Reconciling who the Lord calls me to be within the expectations of the world, the work world in particular, is challenging. Conditions are not such that make living out biblical principles easy. The culture in which I work leaves little room for anything other than working at a mind-numbing rate. Spending any amount of time building relationships with a coworker is frowned upon.

Demands are so great the work is never accomplished, deadlines are often missed, and it seems as though the harder I work the more work is given to me.

One troubling expectation is to consistently work more then the standard forty-hour workweek. Breaks are unheard of. Regular lunch hours away from the desk are taboo; even on the days I don't have a lunch-hour meeting. Yes, I did mention meetings on he lunch hour. It seems we've run out of places to extend our days; we are already coming in early and staying late, and now it's acceptable to schedule meetings on the lunch hour.

There is no recognition or respect for work and life balance where I live in corporate America. I recently heard a leader say that work-life balance is a myth. That saddened me. I disagree. I believe God wants us to live a healthy life-style, giving our time and attention to many things outside of work.

When I find myself wondering what I'm doing in such a place, God reminds me that He's placed me there for His purpose.

> *When he had finished speaking, he said to Simon, "Put out into deep water, and let down the nets for a catch." Simon answered, "Master, we've worked hard all night and haven't caught anything. But because you say so, I will let down the nets." When they had done so, they caught such a large number of fish that their nets began to break.*
>
> *Luke 5: 4-6*

When I am where God has asked me to be, even if I don't see the reason for being there, God is working—through me, in me, and on me. I need to "cast my net" wherever He tells me and trust the results to Him who called me there.

I grow weary. But God's word spurs me on.

> *Let us not become weary in doing good, for at the proper time we will reap a harvest if we do not give up. Therefore, as we have opportunity, let us do good to all people, especially to those who belong to the family of believers.*
>
> *Galatians 6: 9-10*

God has strategically placed you for His purpose in your workplace. Perhaps in striving to be different—healthier—we can model a behavior that will influence others. You may grow weary, but don't give up.

Flowers and Weeds

"*Y*ou are a flower with such a sweet, wonderful fragrance! I bet that's how people feel when they see you in the workplace," my friend exuberantly proclaimed. While I appreciated her sincere compliment, I cringed inside knowing it wasn't always true.

Confessing to her that I'd encountered plenty of people in my workplace that found me anything but a flower wasn't easy. My experience has always been that some people don't like happy, positive people. My guess is that people who feel poorly about themselves are the people who most frequently react negatively when my gregarious personality comes on the scene. As I talked to my friend, I thought of negative coworkers as being like weeds in the garden of work.

> *But thanks be to God, who always leads us in triumphal procession in Christ and through us spreads everywhere the fragrance of the knowledge of him. For we are to God the aroma of Christ among those who are being saved and those who are perishing.*
>
> *2 Corinthians 2:14-15*

Thinking of a particular co-worker who was reacting negatively towards me, knowing that everyone does not know God, I thought to ask my friend to pray. Prayer is always the right answer in every work predicament, just as it is in every life situation. I asked her to pray that I would have compassion for those who don't know Christ. It seemed certain to me those appearing so overwhelmed with negativity must not have a relationship with Him.

In the Bible, the apostle Paul talks about the aroma Christians bring with us when he writes:

> *To the one we are the smell of death; to the other, the fragrance of life. And who is equal to such a task?*
> *2 Corinthians 2:16*

While weeds in a garden attempt to choke the life out of the healthy plants, flowers should breed life, demonstrating peace, love and joy.

> *But the fruit of the Spirit is love, joy, peace, patience, kindness, goodness, faithfulness, gentleness, and self-control . . .*
> *Galatians 5:22-23*

As a Christian, I bring that certain fragrance to my workplace—it is a something that not everyone will like. Accepting this can be hard. Like Paul asks, who is up to the task? I must strive to be a Christ-like presence in the face of negativity and adversity.

> *And so we know and rely on the love God has for us. God is love. Whoever lives in love lives in God, and God in him.*
> *1 John 4:16*

God is love. He is in the garden with us, with the power to transform us. God can help me in the garden.

My friend's encouraging reply to my confession was, "Stand firm and confident in who you are and enjoy the garden for all its magnificent glory, weeds and all, knowing you are beautiful!"

> *Moses answered the people, 'Do not be afraid. Stand firm and you will see the deliverance the Lord will bring you today. The Egyptians you see today you will never see again. The Lord will fight for you; you need only to be still.*
>
> *Exodus 14:13-14*

Bloom where the Lord has planted you—bloom for Him. Stand firm in His glory and don't let the negativity of others cause you to wilt.

God is with you. Love is walking in the garden with you.

Garden of Love

few days after writing about flowers and weeds in the garden of work, a quote about flowers came across my desk through a weekly e-mail subscription.

"Weeds are flowers too, once you get to know them."
A. Milne (Creator of Winnie-the-Pooh)

The words convicted me of speaking too harshly of coworkers when I compared them to weeds.

The extreme negativity in my office was casting long, dark shadows across the department, and I was letting the situation affect my mood and behavior. God showed me, through Milne's quote, that I was guilty of demonstrating the same behaviors I was judging others for. It made me stop and think. Deep reflection left me with two further thoughts:

1. Before God changed me into a flower, I was a weed.
2. Although I thought of myself as a flower, I was just as capable of looking and acting like weed as the next person in the office.

Wow. Realizing and admitting this was hard.

I had spoken harshly of weeds negatively impacting others in the garden of work when I was guilty of being a weed too. According to my own criteria, being a flower required me to positively affect my co-workers. I was not meeting this standard. It is especially important for flowers to have a positive attitude towards weeds because, like the quote correctly stated, they are flowers too.

A flower just waiting for encouragement to blossom lives deep inside everyone. It is important for me to be an encourager.

It's a good thing I'm not alone in the workplace. God is there to help me fulfill my role.

"I am the true vine, and my Father is the gardener."
John 15:1

Our workplace is God's "Garden of Love" and the Gardner is there working on us all. We must be willing to let God change us and not be concerned about changing others.

The work is often dirty in the Garden of Love. This work can expose our hearts and they can be hurt in the process. We need to be willing.

"He cuts off every branch in me that bears no fruit, while every branch that does bear fruit he prunes so that it will be even more fruitful."
John 15:2

It's hard to love people who are insensitive and unkind. Yet, that is what we are called to do. Loving those that are hard to love is part of the process God uses to change us. Pruning is painful, but part of the procedure. God will cut pride and other negative attitudes from us. We need to be open to the process.

Some people have been so hurt they put up a prickly exterior to keep others away. This gives the appearance of being an undesirable weed when nothing could be further from the truth—we are really beautiful, wonderfully made children of God.

God loves us all.

We can't change the weeds; only the Holy Spirit can transform. We can be careful to stay out of His way and not cause harm. We can show compassion and grace, just as our Father has shown us. We are all flowers in God's Garden of Love.

Peace and Good Will

*H*enry Longfellow penned the poem, which was later put to music, *I Heard the Bells on Christmas Day* (1864). He wrote, "In despair I bowed my head: 'There is no peace on earth,' I said, 'For hate is strong and mocks the song . . . '" Longfellow wrote those words during the Civil War, a time in history where our great nation was at war against itself. We can only imagine the anguish this must have caused in men's hearts.

Yet somehow when he heard the bells on Christmas day he heard them proclaiming that peace on earth and good will to men were not dead, nor was God. There was hope in Longfellow's heart.

Discord and hate seem to run rampant in our society today too. War ravages many countries; brave men and women from the United States are involved in these wars as well.

We read of disagreements in the newspaper on a daily basis. On a smaller scale, I see anger and bitterness playing out in the workplace.

What causes fights and quarrels among you? Don't they come from your desires that battle within you? You want something but don't get it.

You kill and covet, but you cannot have what you want. You quarrel and fight. You do not have, because you do not ask God.

James 4: 1-2

We are all individuals, created with unique personalities. We can have different viewpoints and different religions. We can even disagree; but we don't have to fight, hate, and war against each other. We can live in peace, extending good will to one another if we choose to do so.

I'm privileged to be a part of the Christian group in my workplace, and I'm pleased this is a group of men and women who purpose to love all. Peace and good will were demonstrated in my work when the Christian group and the Muslim group joined together to sponsor an event. Sure, the two groups have different viewpoints; but that didn't separate us. We came together to sponsor an event on a subject we agreed on, bringing awareness to employees on depression, and did not focus on our differing viewpoints.

The speaker of the event shared his thirty-year journey with depression. His story was inspirational, and well received by the audience.

The real story was in how diverse employees can work together. The event was so seamless that this part of the story seemed to be missed. That it wasn't an issue or even apparent was part of the beauty.

It was a great example of peace on earth and good will to men. The event was a groundbreaking partnership forged in the workplace, an example for other companies to model—an example for people to follow in all aspects of life.

God desires peace on earth and good will for men. We need to desire the same. We need to make the choice to embrace each other with our differences. It's possible to find things to agree on.

> *Suddenly a great company of the heavenly host appeared with the angel, praising God and saying, "Glory to God in the highest, and on earth peace to men on whom his favor rests."*
>
> *Luke 2: 13-14*

We need to pray and ask God for peace and good will. It's attainable with His help.

Have You Lost Weight?

"Have you lost weight?" It was the third time that week someone had asked me the same question. When I tried to say I hadn't, she insisted on telling me how good I looked without the weight. I wasn't able to argue with her. I walked away smiling to myself and wondering why so many people felt compelled to comment on how well I looked when the answer dawned on me.

A spiritual heaviness had recently been lifted from me. The difference was in my countenance. My step was lighter, my smile was brighter, and a real spiritual oppression was gone. People were seeing something different—they just didn't understand it; therefore, they put a label on the change that they could grasp.

While I needed to lose a few pounds, I had not lost any. My scale measures my weight quite objectively, leaving no room for doubt.

"Come to me, all you who are weary and burdened, and I will give you rest. Take my yoke upon you and learn from me, for I am gentle and humble in heart, and you will find rest for your souls. For my yoke is easy and my burden is light."

Matthew 11: 28-30

When I don't give my burdens to the Lord they become very heavy to carry, even visually weighing me down. Add negative coworkers to the load and my shoulders sag even more. My chin nearly touches the ground, and there is little or no discernable difference between me and my coworkers who do not have faith.

I had been carrying burdens that did not belong to me for far too long—long enough that the "weight" I was bearing had become noticeable.

There is plenty of negativity in the workplace today. The economic climate is putting additional demands on organizations and employees are feeling it.

A conscious effort is required to fight the battle and to keep the negativity others are wishing to share from creeping into our souls. The enemy is making a bid for our peace, and he is doing it through the workplace.

> **Put on the full armor of God so that you can take your stand against the devil's schemes. For our struggle is not against flesh and blood, but against the rulers, against the authorities, against the powers of this dark world and against the spiritual forces of evil in the heavenly realms.**
>
> **Ephesians 6: 11-12**

Shed some spiritual weight by giving your burdens to God and by taking your stand today. See if your coworkers comment on your weight loss.

CHAPTER SIX

Compassion

A Welcoming Smile

*F*rom across the long hallway she looked like a beacon of light marking a safe harbor. Although I didn't know her well, I knew her as a kind person and I decided to head her way.

As I drew near, she looked up with spark of light in her eyes that said she was glad to see me; kindness and compassion were unmistakably behind the light.

My coworker was sitting on the stairway reviewing her notes before an early morning presentation. We greeted each other warmly.

I felt like I could have laid my head on her shoulder and told her how I was really feeling. My weekend was challenging. I was hit hard with two family emergencies in the span of the same weekend. One was a death. It was Monday morning and my coworker could have had no idea how tough my weekend had been or how desperately I needed a friendly face.

It's like that in the workplace; we often have no idea what the next person is going through outside of work.

I was feeling the double whammy more than she could have known. I didn't rest my head on her shoulders that morning on the steps, but I appreciate that I could have. She only had a short time before her presentation, and it wouldn't have been appropriate for me to share with her at that moment.

However, I did catch up with her later and let her know I was hurting and how much I appreciated her welcoming smile.

The workplace isn't always compassion-friendly or inviting on a personal level. Even when we have people who care, the environment isn't necessarily conducive for personal relationships. We rush through our busy days, sometimes in a blur, without remembering to ask one another how we are really doing. Oh, sure, on a Monday morning the greeting for the new workweek might include an inquiry as to how we are. But, there's a certain expectation for us to reply with the cursory "fine."

Jesus showed kindness and compassion wherever He went. We should model His behavior.

> *When Jesus landed and saw a large crowd, he had compassion on them and healed their sick.*
> *Matthew 14:14*

A little kindness and compassion can make a big difference. Something as simple as a welcoming smile could make a great difference in another person's day. A coworker might be hurting, and you may not know it. Exemplifying compassion in the workplace is showing God's love and has healing power. You could be a beacon of light in your workplace today, and it just may start with a simple smile.

Mercy and Compassion

I encouraged my son to believe the best in another by extending mercy and compassion in a work situation he didn't understand. It was good advice.

Walking away I wondered what would happen if I took my advice in a similar work situation. It seemed like I should be willing to practice what I preached to my son. I decided I would make an effort to be compassionate and forgiving too.

I had also been judgmental toward a coworker. This person had hurt me deeply, both personally and professionally. I needed to consider the possibility that there was not ill intent behind her words and actions.

I needed to offer the same mercy and compassion I was advising my son to use. After all, God has been generous, showing me mercy and compassion; therefore, I needed to do the same.

We all will experience difficult situations in the workplace.

> *"I have told you these things, so that in me you may have peace. In this world you will have trouble. But take heart! I have overcome the world."*
>
> ### *John 16:33*

Knowing tough work situations will come, we can take comfort in knowing that with Jesus we can have peace in the middle of them.

The situation provided me with a seemingly insurmountable challenge—the call to rise above difficulty and show Christ-like behavior. Although I went back to work bolstered and encouraged I was not able to meet my challenge. I was not able to reach out in love and attempt reconciliation. I was still too hurt.

In despair I came down hard on myself for not being able to do what was right. The experience showed me that I needed to extend mercy and compassion to my own troubled heart before I could share the same with others.

> *Not that I have already obtained all this, or have already been made perfect, but I press on to take hold of that for which Christ Jesus took hold of me. Brothers, I do not consider myself yet to have taken hold of it. But one thing I do: Forgetting what is behind and straining toward what is ahead, I press on toward the goal to win the prize for which God has called me heavenward in Christ Jesus.*
>
> *Philippians 3:12-14*

Paul wrote about wanting to do one thing and not being able to do it either. Take encouragement in his words. Give yourself mercy and compassion when you are not able to measure up to your expectations and continue to press on.

Only by God's Grace

*I*knew I should report my coworker; but I knew reporting her would result in serious consequences for her. It was likely she would lose her job. My coworker had committed a serious infraction against me. How this type of offense could happen in the workplace was beyond belief. I was so shocked by what had happened that I didn't know how to respond.

Stop and pray. It was the only thing I could think to do. My mind was reeling. I didn't have peace about going to the authorities and I had no idea how to confront her. Doing nothing, even temporarily, seemed outlandish. I didn't know what else to do.

I went home that evening without any clear direction of how to proceed, and I returned to work the next day still not knowing how to handle the situation.

Tension hung thick in the air. As uncomfortable as I was, I couldn't imagine how much more the situation might be affecting my coworker. She and I sat close to each other. The morning progressed without a break in the situation.

Just before lunch my coworker asked to talk to me. She tearfully apologized for what she had done.

I accepted her apology, and with God's grace I forgave her. I didn't mention it again—not to her or to anyone in authority.

> **Be kind and compassionate to one another, forgiving each other, just as in Christ God forgave you.**
>
> **Ephesians 4:32**

My coworker knew she didn't deserve my grace or forgiveness. By the same token I know I do not deserve God's grace and compassion either. Yet He freely and frequently lavishes these gifts on me, just as he does on everyone of us. What a gift these things are!

God gave me the grace to remain silent. God gave me the grace to forgive her. I couldn't have done these things in my own power; my response was only because of God's grace. This demonstration of grace transformed my coworker. Her demeanor changed, not just towards me, but towards others as well. She became my friend, my very grateful friend.

I am grateful for God's grace in my life; it is a grace I need to bring to work and freely share with others each day. This kind of grace comes from God through prayer.

God's grace has changed me. It has allowed me to do things I would never have thought possible, and wouldn't be on my own. When I allow God's grace to flow through me, others are impacted as well.

CHAPTER SEVEN

Trust

Unbeknownst to Me

$\mathcal{U}$nexpectedly unemployed for the fourth time in my career and feeling extremely discouraged, I trudged through the motions of a job search. Wondering and waiting were part of the process, but not new to me. I knew the drill too well. I remembered that a respected mentor in the workplace once told me that perfectly good people get dislocated through no fault of their own in a bad economy. He counseled me saying that employers recognized this and were not only willing to hire people who had been laid-off, but often looked to them as desirable people to hire.

I took some comfort in remembering his wise counsel, but it was still hard place to be.

I targeted a large and highly respected organization in my community. It wasn't an easy target; it was one of those places everyone wanted to work. When an opportunity came, it was not in the form I had expected or hoped for—it came through an entry-level position.

Not being sure I wanted to step as far back in my career as an entry-level job would cause me to, I had to pause and gauge my desire to get into the company. While there were no guarantees of security anywhere, in comparison to the smaller companies I'd been employed by, this company seemed like it would be a much more stable place to work. Stability was very alluring with four dislocations under my belt. I thought a company of that size would be a land of opportunity with a chance to move into a new position in a short amount of time. After deciding the benefits outweighed the sacrifices, I accepted the position. It felt like a door that God wanted me to step through.

It wasn't long before I doubted my decision. The position wasn't a good fit for me. While I could easily do the job, I felt confined, undervalued and unappreciated. Coming to work was drudgery. My attitude sank to the bottom of the pit, making the drive to work less appealing every day.

While my work record had been stellar at every company I'd ever worked for in my entire life, my performance came under question, which devastated me even more. I was not in a good place.

I was absolved from the false accusations surrounding my work performance, and two years after starting the entry-level job I found another position within the company. While this job and the other three subsequent jobs were much better, I knew each step was still on my way to somewhere else, and I moved on quickly searching for the right place.

Six and a half years and five positions later, I arrived at the perfect place for me. At last, it felt like a place I was supposed to be, versus always a place on the way to somewhere else. It was the place that, unbeknownst to me, God had been moving me toward the whole time. We say hindsight is 20/20, and an opportunity to look back does indeed bring clarity to vision. Now I could see how each experience, especially the toughest ones, were preparing me for the places God had in mind for me all along.

When I started at the company in that entry-level job I didn't even know where I wanted to go. I had a vague, general idea of where I thought I should go. The field I ended up in was not area I'd ever heard of, but much to my delight discovered along the way. The journey was rich, but I wasn't wise enough to recognize the beauty along the way; I was always too intent on getting to my undefined destination.

Of course I'm still on the journey; we will always be on the way to where God is leading us. But I'm in a really good place now. I feel energized by work I find fascinating. I'm learning. I'm challenged. I feel like I found a home, and I'm working in a much healthier work group with encouraging people again.

I couldn't see the plan from the first department where I started, nor could I see it in the next few places.

I did not know I could get here from there. In fact, I could never have even guessed it. But, God knew. He knew every often, painful step there was a reason for every place and every experience.

God has a plan. He always had a plan. The many challenges along the way prepared me to be able to be where I am today. Unbeknownst to me, God was moving in the right direction all the time.

And we know that in all things God works for the good of those who love him, who have been called according to his purpose.

Romans 8:28

It's a story about trusting God, trusting even when we can't see where we are going, trusting He is moving us and preparing us for where He wants us to be. God can use every step we take.

God's Timing—Not Mine

*T*hree years of working hard to see results of the vision had brought nothing—not one single opportunity had came from all my labor. When it was God's timing, He brought three opportunities within a three-week period of time.

Working with the Christian group in my workplace for a number of years had been richly rewarding. Being part of a successful launch and start-up was the answer to many prayers. Desiring to see such groups at other companies drove me out into the community to stir up interest. I didn't find any.

Certain this vision was from God, I hastily developed a plan and went about execution. I forgot an important element of success—God's timing.

> *Delight yourself in the Lord and he will give you the desires of your heart.*
>
> *Psalm 37:4*

God does give us the desires of our heart only to fulfill those desires. However, God does this in His time, not ours. It does not work when we try to choose the time.

Try as I might, I couldn't make any connections in the community. I knew I had the right idea and continued to plunge ahead with any fruits of my labor.

> **Unless the Lord builds the house, its builders labor in vain. Unless the Lord watches over the city, the watchmen stand guard in vain.**
>
> **Psalm 127:1**

It is important to wait for God. As in this case, working on my own timetable does not produce results. Although I had the right plan, I had not waited for God to open the doors and oversee the project. Waiting for God once He gives the game plan can be challenging if you are not a patient person. God was trying to teach me to be patient.

> **. . . but those who hope in the Lord will renew their strength. They will soar on wings like eagles; they will run and not grow weary, they will walk and not be faint.**
>
> **Isaiah 40:31**

I waited for God, not because I was wise enough at the time to recognize what was happening, but because I was exhausted. The opportunities came when I least expected it, when I was too weary to continue on in my own strength.

The connections God brought were not small ones—they were three inquiries from major organizations in our city. After years of trying, they came within three weeks of each other.

God brought the opportunities (not to me, but to our group) and blessed us by letting us work alongside three new Christian groups in our community.

Bringing my faith to the workplace has been rewarding beyond anything I could ever have imagined. It gives me great pleasure to serve the Lord in the workplace. Learning to wait for God has been a valuable lesson.

I'm Still Here

*M*y favorite author and speaker, Joyce Meyer, has been known to say that her testimony is, "I'm still here." I understand that message.

I'm still here too. Still standing. It's been a long, winding, uphill road. Navigating through corporate America has been challenging for me. If you have found the workplace to be challenging, I want you to know you're not alone.

I wasn't young and inexperienced when I entered the corporate America door; yet I was still met with more uphill struggles than I ever could have imagined.

I often wonder, *What if I would have quit when the going got tough?*

Only a couple of twists and turns down the way I wasn't sure if I was going to make it. "The first five years are the toughest," a good friend told me. I thought, *You don't understand, I won't be here in five years.* I merely smiled at her, too weary to argue.

After nearly seven years I finally arrived in a better place. However, much to my surprise a challenge erupted like a volcano reminding me it was still the corporate work setting. A previous manager, with a personal vendetta, struck unexpectedly. I had only been in my new position for a few days! I didn't even see trouble coming. I'm thankful I had a good boss to help me manage. The reminder was very real.

Jesus never promised an easy life. He said there would be challenges along the way.

> *"I have told you these things, so that in me you may have peace. In this world you will have trouble. But take heart! I have overcome the world."*
>
> *John 16:33*

There is no peace—no real, lasting peace—in the world, only in Jesus Christ, the Lord and Savior.

> *Brothers and sisters, I do not consider myself yet to have taken hold of it. But one thing I do: Forgetting what is behind and straining toward what is ahead, I press on toward the goal to win the prize for which God has called me heavenward in Christ Jesus.*
>
> *Philippians 3:13-14*

The workplace has provided me with many challenges. Each new struggle has been an opportunity for growth. God is using the workplace to change and refine me.

I'm still here—still at the company that has been a hard place for to be for many years. I'm extremely blessed to be in a better place now. I'm extremely grateful that God has brought me to a new place and put me under the care of good manager. I'm thankful for emotionally stable, healthy teammates.

I'm very grateful to my current manager for restoring my faith in the corporate world and for giving me a hope that we can all make a difference and make our places of work better.

No matter where you are today, I hope this encourages you and gives you hope.

God walks through the marketplace with us. He is greater than any work challenge we will ever face. Wherever life finds you today, please be encouraged.

Afterwards

Thank you for taking the time to read my book. I pray God has used my stories to give you hope and encouragement on your journey. God uses every circumstance in our life to transform us into the men and women He created us to be. I can't think of any place I spend more of my time than the workplace. It's important to me to bring my faith to work with me and to encourage you to do the same.

I haven't always made good choices, as these stories show. However, God has always been there, always faithful. I feel that God has asked me to be real, transparent, and authentic with my life and these stories in order to encourage you.

I'm still learning, and I will be until the day Jesus calls me home to be with Him. I believe we can learn much from each other and in sharing our stories of faith. I would love to hear from you if there was something in my book that encouraged you or if you have a story of faith you would like to share. Please visit my website!

www.sharijharris.com

About the Author

Shari lives in Minneapolis, Minnesota with her husband, Bill. She has been in the workplace since her first job at Bressler's 33 Flavors Ice Cream Shop in Minneapolis in 1977.

Shari's life was touched and forever changed when a coworker shared her faith in Jesus Christ with her in the workplace. Shari committed her life to Christ and entered into a relationship with Jesus. Because of this life-changing event, Shari is passionate about being a Christian in the workplace and sharing her faith.

Shari holds a B.S. in Business Management from Northwestern College, Roseville, Minnesota. She has served on the leadership council of the Christian employee group for over seven years in a variety of roles and is a past Chairperson. She served as a deaconess on her church board for six years.

Shari writes, speaks, and teaches passionately on faith in the workplace. She is an Apprentice in the Christian Writer's Guild. Shari has written for the Examiner.com and Workplace Influence. She has also written a blog about her mother's journey with ALS (Lou Gehrigs disease). http://sharijoysblog.blogspot.com/

www.sharijharris.com

Notes

1. Krippayne, S. (1995). *Sometimes He Calms the Storm* on *Wild Imaginations* Audio CD.

2. Blanchard, K. & Hodges, P. (2005). *Lead Like Jesus: Lessons For Everyone From The Greatest Leadership Role Model of All Times.* Nashville: Thomas Nelson.

3. Nouwen, H.J.M. (1992) *In the Name of Jesus: Reflections on Christian Leadership.* New York: Crossroad.

4. Walsh, S. (2009). *Beautiful Things Happen When a Woman Trusts God.* Nashville: Thomas Nelson.

CPSIA information can be obtained at www.ICGtesting.com
226575LV00001B/3/P